Bible Stories for Children
The
Old Testament

Retold by Vic Parker

Miles
KeLLY

First published in 2010 by Miles Kelly Publishing Ltd
Harding's Barn, Bardfield End Green, Thaxted, Essex, CM6 3PX, UK

Copyright © Miles Kelly Publishing Ltd 2010

This edition published in 2011

2 4 6 8 10 9 7 5 3 1

Publishing Director Belinda Gallagher
Creative Director Jo Cowan
Editor Carly Blake
Designers Michelle Foster, Joe Jones
Cover/Design Kayleigh Allen
Consultant Janet Dyson
Production Manager Elizabeth Collins
Reprographics Stephan Davis, Ian Paulyn

ISBN 978-1-84810-530-0

Printed in China

British Library Cataloguing-in-Publication Data
A catalogue record for this book is available from the British Library

ACKNOWLEDGEMENTS
The publishers would like to thank the following artists
who have contributed to this book:

The Bright Agency Katriona Chapman, Dan Crisp,
Giuliano Ferri (inc. cover), Mélanie Florian

Advocate Art Andy Catling, Alida Massari

*The publishers would like to thank Robert Willoughby and
the London School of Theology for their help in compiling this book.*

Made with paper from a sustainable forest
www.mileskelly.net
info@mileskelly.net

www.factsforprojects.com

Contents

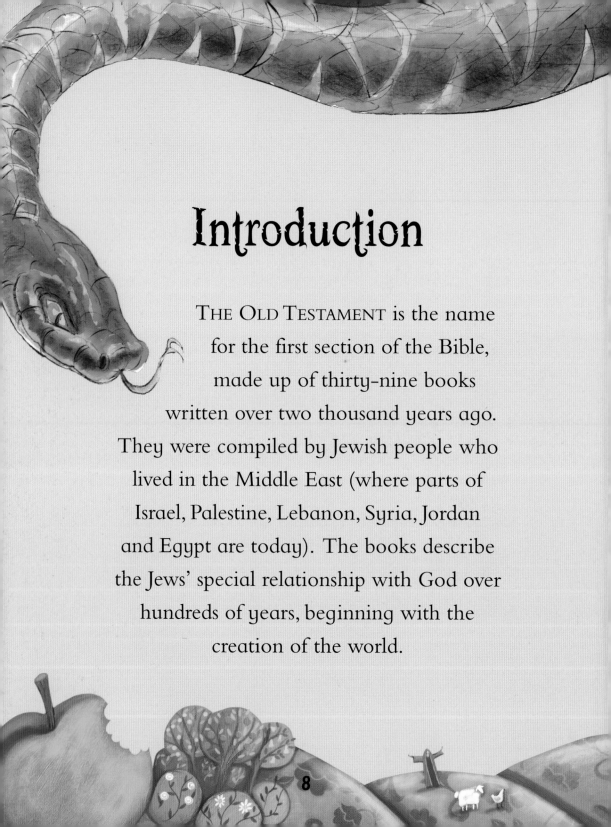

Introduction

THE OLD TESTAMENT is the name
for the first section of the Bible,
made up of thirty-nine books
written over two thousand years ago.
They were compiled by Jewish people who
lived in the Middle East (where parts of
Israel, Palestine, Lebanon, Syria, Jordan
and Egypt are today). The books describe
the Jews' special relationship with God over
hundreds of years, beginning with the
creation of the world.

The Jews made many careful copies of the original ancient manuscripts, so the writings of the Old Testament were never lost. They contain family trees, religious laws, poetry, hymns and stories that narrate events surrounding hundreds of characters.

At the beginning of each story is a short introduction. This helps to set the scene by providing information about the time period, events and characters.

The Creation of the World

The first book of the Bible is called Genesis, which means 'beginning', and the first story tells how God created the world. Everything was perfect and God was pleased with His creation, but things did not stay this way for long.

In the beginning, God lived in darkness. There was nothing else except for a vast ocean that rushed and raged over a mass of land that lay beneath. Then God had an idea. "Let there be light!" He said, and mysteriously there was. God liked the brightness. He enjoyed it for a while and then called the darkness back for another turn. That was the very first day and night.

When God lit up the second day He had another idea. "I want a roof to arch over everything, way up high!" He said, and all at once there was one. Then He parted the ocean, scooped up half of the water and poured it out onto the roof. The swirling patterns that formed above were beautiful. God gave the roof a special name – sky.

God looked down at the remaining water boiling and bubbling below. "Move aside so the land can show through!" He ordered, and it did. The land rose up and the water swirled around it. God was very pleased and decided to call them earth and sea. But He thought the land looked too bare. God imagined grass and flowers and bushes and trees. Before the third day ended, they were growing all over the earth.

On day number four, God decorated the sky. In it He hung a blazing, hot light called the sun, a pale, cold light called the moon and millions of burning, twinkling stars. Then He set them all moving around each other in a way that would mark out the passing of the days, nights, seasons and years.

Next, God looked over His creation and decided that He wanted things to live in it. He spent the fifth day imagining all sorts of creatures that floated, swam and dived in the water, and that soared, hovered and buzzed in the air. Suddenly, the sea was

13

filled with fish and sea creatures and the air was busy with birds and insects.

On the sixth day, God imagined creatures that galloped, hopped and slithered. Creatures with fur, scales and shells, and with claws, hooves and horns. Creatures that barked, hissed, howled and grunted. All at once, the earth was alive with all kinds of animals.

Last of all, God took a handful of earth and modelled it into a figure that looked just like Him. He bent down and breathed into the figure's nostrils and it shivered, blinked and came alive, and looked at Him. It was the first man, Adam.

God quickly realized that the man would be lonely all on his own, so He sent Adam into a deep sleep while He made him a companion. God gently took out one of the man's ribs and healed up the wound. Then He shaped the rib into another, similar figure – the first woman, Eve. Finally, God brought Eve to life, then woke up Adam and introduced them to each other. God watched His two humans with delight as they spoke and got to know each other. God was so thrilled with them that He put them in charge of all the other living things He had made. He even planted a beautiful garden especially for Adam and Eve to live in, in a place called Eden.

At last, God sat back and looked at the world He had created. He had used every colour, shape and texture, and every size,

sound and scent that He could think of.
God was very pleased with everything, and
decided that He had done enough. He spent
the seventh day relaxing after all His efforts.
God ordered that from then on, every
seventh day should be a special day of rest
in memory of when He had completed His
wonderful work.

And that is how the world was made.

Genesis chapters 1, 2

Adam and Eve in the Garden of Eden

This story is about the first man and woman and how they lived in paradise in the Garden of Eden. One day Eve, then Adam, was tempted to disobey God. Because of this, evil and suffering came into the world and Adam and Eve were sent to live among it.

God made sure that the Garden of Eden had everything that Adam and Eve needed to be happy. The sun kept them warm, so they didn't need clothes – they weren't embarrassed about being naked anyway. A gushing stream gave them water. All sorts of flowers, plants and trees grew

there, fragrant and shady, and
bearing tasty fruits, nuts and seeds.
In the middle of the garden grew the
two most beautiful trees of all – the Tree
of Life and the Tree of Knowledge.

"Take care of my marvellous garden,"
God told Adam and Eve. "Enjoy eating
anything you like, except for the fruits of
the Tree of Knowledge. Please do not eat
those. If you do, you will die."

Adam and Eve did as they were told and
their life in the garden was wonderful, until
one day Eve met a snake. The snake was by
far the most cunning of all the creatures
God had made. Very slyly, it asked Eve,
"Did God really tell you not to eat from
one of the trees?"

"Yes, that one," replied Eve, pointing to the Tree of Knowledge. "He said that if we do, we'll die. I don't think we're even allowed to touch it."

"Nonsense," hissed the snake. "You won't die! God doesn't want you to eat that fruit because if you do, you'll become like Him. You'll know the difference between good and bad, just as He does."

Eve gazed nervously at the Tree of Knowledge. How beautiful it was! Its leaves whispered mysteriously in the breeze and its branches stretched towards her. Its fruits hung down, ripe and ready to drop into her hand. "How wonderful it would be to become wise!" Eve murmured.

Overcome with longing, she reached out, picked the nearest fruit and took a big, juicy bite. It was so delicious! Surely something that tasted so good could not be wrong. Eve hurried to share the fruit with Adam and he couldn't resist trying it either.

Suddenly, Adam and Eve realized that they did indeed know the difference between good and bad – and what they had done was very wrong. The couple felt dreadfully ashamed and were embarrassed about being naked too. They tried to sew leaves together to cover themselves. Then, in horror, they heard God coming. Quickly, they hid, but God knew.

"Adam," God called, "why are you and Eve hiding from me?"

The red-faced couple crept out, hanging their heads.

"We were frightened when we heard you, and also we weren't dressed," Adam mumbled.

"What has made you want clothes? And why are you afraid of me?" God demanded. "You haven't eaten the fruit I asked you not to eat, have you?"

Adam owned up, but he blamed it all on Eve, who in turn blamed the snake. God listened as they squirmed and squabbled. Then with huge disappointment He said,

"I have no choice but to punish you all."

He sent the snake crawling away in the dust, the enemy of humans forever. After making animal-skin clothes for Adam and Eve, He turned them out of their beautiful garden home. "From now on, you will have to fend for yourselves and struggle to grow your own food," God told them. "And one day, you will go back to being the earth from which I made you – you will one day die." He set angels with fiery swords to guard the Tree of Life, so that Adam and Eve could not eat its fruit to save themselves from eventually dying. God watched in great sadness as the shamed couple walked out into the world.

Genesis chapters 2, 3

Noah's Ark

In the world that God had made, people began to be wicked.
God was sad and angry at mankind and decided to wipe
every person from the face of the Earth. But one man,
Noah, was good and he loved God. He and his family
were given a very special task.

As the years went by, Adam and Eve had many great-grandchildren who had many great-great-grandchildren of their own. People spread all over the world. They quite forgot that they were part of one big family. They also forgot about God and began behaving badly in lots of ways.

God looked down from Heaven and became more and more sad and angry. Eventually, people became so selfish and cruel that God was sorry He had ever created the human race. He decided the best thing was to remove everybody and start all over again.

Well, not quite everybody. There was just one person in the world who tried to live a good, honest, hard-working life – a farmer called Noah. God decided to save Noah, his wife and three sons, Shem, Ham and Japheth, and their wives.

God spoke to Noah and told him about His terrible decision. "Look around you, Noah. Everyone in the world is evil, and I have had enough. I am going to wash everybody off the face of the earth, but I promise, you and your family will be safe.

"Here's what you have to do. I want you to build a huge, covered boat – an ark. Use the best wood you can find and build it 133 metres long, 22 metres wide and 13 metres high, with a roof of reeds. Coat the whole thing with tar, inside and out, so that it is watertight. Give it a door and windows and build three decks divided into compartments. When I tell you, load up the ark with one pair of every living creature – a male and a female. Take seven pairs of animals you can eat because you'll need enough food to feed you all. I am going to send forty days and forty nights of rain to flood the whole world."

Noah told his family and they hurried to begin the enormous task. Their neighbours thought they were mad as they began building the huge ship. How people laughed! But Noah and his family trusted God and kept working, and after many months the ark was finished. The day came when God warned Noah to begin loading the animals into the ark and settling his family onboard. A week later, thunder clouds blackened the skies, blotting out the sun, and it began to rain.

Genesis chapters 6, 7

The Great Flood

The flood waters washed away all of the evil that was in the world, leaving it fresh and clean so that Noah and his family could make a new beginning. The rainbow and the olive branch have become symbols of hope and peace.

The rain that God sent to flood the world was like nothing anyone had seen before or could have imagined. It was as if the sky had shattered and through the cracks plunged mighty waterfalls. As the rain poured down, rivers burst their banks, lakes flooded their valleys, oceans swelled and overflowed and the ark floated off on the rising waters. Towering tidal waves rushed over the land, drowning everything in their path, and still the rain continued. The ark was lashed and battered, and hurled this way and that by the currents.

The rain fell for forty days and nights just as God had said. Then as quickly as it had started, it stopped. When Noah dared to peep out, he could see nothing but water in all directions.

Over the quiet, empty days that followed, the sun began to dry up the water and the flood gradually started to sink. God sent a great wind to speed things along. Eventually, the ark groaned and shuddered as it scraped along the ground and came to a halt on top of Mount Ararat in Turkey.

Noah didn't dare leave the ark yet. He waited a few days for the waters to sink further, then sent a raven into the sky. The raven soared back and forth and all it could see was water. Noah waited a week, then sent out a dove. It flew back the same day and Noah knew that there was not enough land showing yet. He waited another week, then sent the dove out again. That evening it returned, carrying an olive leaf. The waters were low enough to show land where trees grew! Noah waited one week more and again sent out the dove. This time it did not return. Nervously, Noah opened the door and the ark was surrounded by dry land!

Then God called, "Noah, it's time for you and your family to go out into the world with the creatures and begin again." And that's what they did. God was pleased and blessed Noah and his family. He vowed that He would never again send a flood to destroy the living things He had created. God set a rainbow in the sky as a sign to always remind everyone of His promise.

Genesis chapters 7 to 9

The Tower of Babel

When God saw that people were building a tower reaching from Earth to Heaven so that they would be known throughout the world for their great city, He put a stop to their plan in an unusual way.

In the early days of the world people lived much longer than they do now. The Bible says that Noah was six hundred years old at the time of the flood and that he didn't die until he was nine hundred and fifty! Noah lived to see his sons and their wives have many children, grandchildren and generations of great-grandchildren. The family grew so big that there were many thousands of people in the world again, just as God had wished.

Of course, people travelled to distant lands to find places to live. Many spent years wandering about, looking for good grazing land for their animals, living in tents that they moved from place to place. As time went on, people in different lands developed different tastes in clothing, cooking and customs, just like today. But one thing they all had in common was the same language.

When one particular group of wanderers arrived at the land of Shinar, which is now called Iraq, they decided to settle on a wide, flat plain. The countryside had everything the travellers could want, and they liked it so much that they decided they would never move on again. The travellers thought hard and came up with a big, bold plan. Instead of living in tents, they would build a lasting home for themselves – a fixed settlement made out of bricks.

They worked out how to make bricks from mud, which they could bake hard and stick together with tar. But the people didn't want to build just a village or a town, they didn't even want to build a city. They wanted to build the grandest, most beautiful city with a tower for a showpiece. A tower so tall that its top would touch the clouds. The settlers wanted news of their

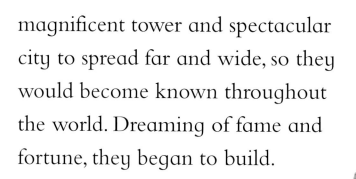

magnificent tower and spectacular
city to spread far and wide, so they
would become known throughout
the world. Dreaming of fame and
fortune, they began to build.

   With all the digging,
moulding, baking, hammering
and chiselling that was going
on, it wasn't long before
God noticed what the
people of Shinar were
doing. He looked down
from Heaven and was
amazed at the pleasing
streets that were being
laid out, the stylish
houses that were

taking shape and the stunning tower that was soaring upwards into the sky. "My goodness!" God said to Himself. "I can't believe what these people are achieving! They're doing a wonderful job." But then a thought struck Him. "Hmmm… the only thing is, they're doing it because they want to be more important than everyone else. If I let them continue like this, they'll get quite carried away. Soon they'll want everything they have to be the biggest and best. I'd better put a stop to it before things get out of hand."

All at once, God gave the people different languages. Suddenly, they all found that they couldn't understand a word each other was saying. Without being able to communicate, their building plans ground to a halt. They couldn't work together to finish the city, which came to be known as Babel, or Babylon, because of the babble of voices inside it. Gradually everyone left Shinar in frustration and went their separate ways, seeking new homes.

From then on, as they settled in distant lands, people in different countries spoke different languages.

Genesis chapter 11

Abram's Journey

The next five stories are about Abraham, Isaac and Jacob – the fathers, or 'patriarchs', of the nation that became Israel. Abram (later called Abraham) obeyed God's command to leave his home and travel to an unknown land. He had no idea where God was leading him, but Abram trusted God.

One of the descendants of Noah's son Shem was a man called Abram. He grew up in a city called Ur, near the Persian Gulf. After Abram married he took his wife, Sarai, his father, Terah, and his orphaned nephew, Lot (whom he had brought up as his own son) to live in a northern city called

Haran. Both Ur and Haran were bustling
places full of wealthy people just like
Abram, who was a successful businessman.
But one day, out of the blue, Abram heard
God calling him.

   "Abram, I want you to leave and
go to the country that I will show
you. I am going to make you
the father of a
great race of
people."

It must
have taken a lot
of faith to do as God
asked. Abram sold most of
his possessions, packed up the rest and set off
with his wife on a long journey without

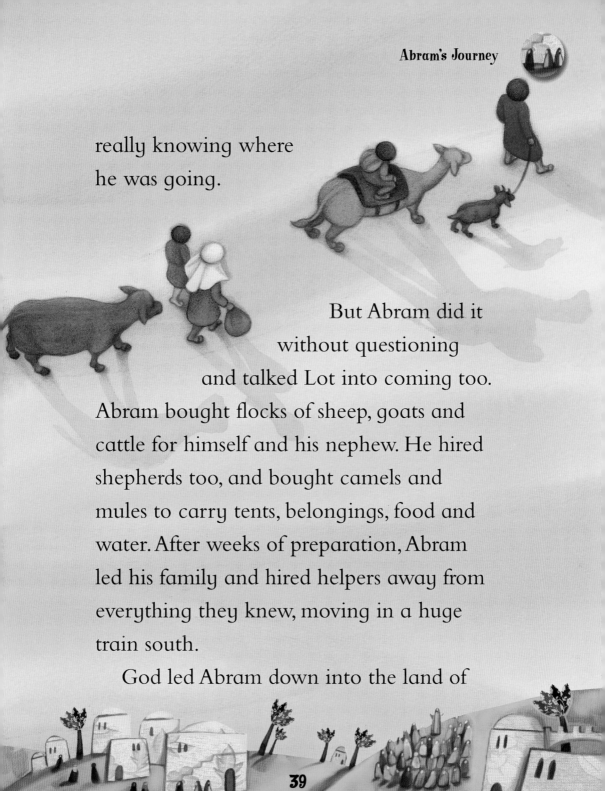

really knowing where
he was going.

But Abram did it
without questioning
and talked Lot into coming too.
Abram bought flocks of sheep, goats and
cattle for himself and his nephew. He hired
shepherds too, and bought camels and
mules to carry tents, belongings, food and
water. After weeks of preparation, Abram
led his family and hired helpers away from
everything they knew, moving in a huge
train south.

God led Abram down into the land of

Canaan, which is now called Israel. When
Abram reached a holy place called
Shechem, he heard God's voice saying,
"This is the country that I am going to give
to your descendants." Descendants! Abram
was mystified. He and his wife Sarai were
well past middle-age and although they
had always longed for a family, they had
never been able to have children. Again,
Abram tried not to question God, but to
trust once more.

They could not stay in Canaan as there
was a terrible famine, so God guided the
family through the desert to the lush land of
Egypt. Here, food and water were plentiful
but Abram found himself in quite another
kind of trouble. Pharaoh, the king of Egypt,

ordered that Sarai had to become one of his wives. So God sent a terrible disease to strike Pharaoh and his advisors until he changed his mind, and he soon let Sarai go.

After that, Abram left Egypt behind and headed north into Canaan again, to a place called Bethel. There wasn't enough grassland for all the animals to graze on, and Abram's and Lot's shepherds began quarrelling and fighting over it. There was only one thing for it – the two men split up.

Lot went east into Jordan where he settled at a city called Sodom, while his uncle unpacked his tents and stayed in the countryside of Canaan. After Lot had left, God spoke to Abram again and repeated his vow. "Look around you," He said. "All this

land as far as the eye can see will belong to you and your family forever."

And so Abram waited… Seasons came and went, but there was still no sign that he and Sarai would ever have children.

Over the years, God spoke to him several times, repeating his promise. It was always when Abram least expected it. One night, Abram was sitting outside his tent as usual when he heard God say, "Look up. You will have as many descendants as there are stars in the sky." Another time, after Abram had made an offering to God, he had a terrifyingly real dream. In it God walked right next to him, vowing again that he would have a vast, wealthy family and that all the land from the River Nile to the

River Euphrates would be theirs.

As time went on, Sarai grew concerned that she would never be able to give Abram a child so she encouraged her eighty-six-year-old husband to have a baby with her maid Hagar, instead. Hagar and Abram had a son called Ishmael, but rather than cheering Sarai up, it plunged her into sadness.

Abram turned ninety-nine years old and Sarai reached ninety, and still they had no child of their own. However God insisted that His promise remained true. "I want you and your wife to change your names as a sign of my vow," He said. "From now on, you will not be Abram and Sarai, but Abraham and Sarah. Do what I say and

trust me, and everything I have told you will come true. You and Sarah will have your own baby next year, you'll see. I want you to call him Isaac."

So Abraham and Sarah continued to wait.

Genesis chapters 11 to 13, 15 to 17

God's Promise Comes True

Eventually, Abraham and Sarah had a child. As God had promised, Abraham's sons became the founders of two great nations – the Hebrews and the Arabs.

At long last, when Abraham was one hundred years old, Sarah had a baby boy whom they called Isaac. Everything had come to pass just as God had said.

The couple were so overjoyed that they thought nothing could spoil their happiness. But gradually, Sarah became eaten up with

envy of Abraham's other son, Ishmael, whom he had with Sarah's maid, Hagar.

There had been trouble between the two women ever since Hagar had become pregnant. Because she was carrying Abraham's baby, Hagar had put on airs and graces and looked down on her mistress. Sarah had become so annoyed that she had treated Hagar badly. So badly that Hagar had eventually run away. An angel found Hagar weeping by a desert spring and comforted her, convincing her to return. God reassured Sarah too. He said that He would make Abraham and Hagar's son, Ishmael, the founder of a great race. But when Abraham and Sarah had a son, Isaac, it would be his descendants who would be God's own special people.

However when Isaac was born, the rivalry Sarah felt towards Hagar brewed again. Ishmael was about fourteen and he was fond of his little brother, but Sarah hated seeing them together. She couldn't stand to be reminded that because both boys had the same father, her maid's son was equally important.

"Get rid of them!" Sarah begged Abraham. "I don't want Ishmael around, taking what should rightfully be Isaac's."

Abraham was upset because he loved both his sons. He asked God what to do.

"Don't worry," God reassured him. "Do as Sarah suggests. I'll look after Hagar and Ishmael. Trust me."

Next morning, Abraham told Hagar that she and Ishmael had to leave. With a heavy heart, he gave them food and a waterskin, and turned them out into the desert.

God kept His word and looked after Abraham's first son and his mother as they struggled to survive on their own. Once, when they were close to dying of thirst, God sent an angel to them with water. God stayed at Ishmael's side as he grew up, and he became strong and brave. Just as God had promised, He made Ishmael the founder of a great nation — the Arabs.

Genesis chapters 16, 17

A Tale of Twin Brothers

*Abraham's son Isaac grew up to have children of his own –
twin boys called Jacob and Esau. Jacob was jealous of Esau
because as the elder son he would inherit his father's wealth.
So Jacob plotted to trick his brother out of his inheritance.*

Isaac's mother, Sarah, lived to be one
hundred and twenty-seven years old,
while his father, Abraham, lived to one
hundred and seventy-five. By the time they
both died, Isaac had married a girl called
Rebecca, from Abraham's old town of
Haran. Isaac inherited his father's farming

business and stayed in Canaan, following God's will just as Abraham had done.

Like Isaac's father and mother, he and Rebecca had to wait a long time before God sent them children – twenty years. It was worth the wait, for when Rebecca finally found herself expecting a baby it was not one, but two – twins! A short time before they were born, God told Rebecca, "You are having two sons, who will lead two peoples. One boy will be stronger than the other and the older one will serve the younger one."

At the birth, a very strange thing happened. The second baby came out holding the first one's heel, as though he wanted to pull his older brother back and overtake. Isaac and Rebecca called the elder boy Esau, because the name means 'hairy' and Esau was dark and had lots of hair. They named their younger, fairer son Jacob, which means 'someone who wants to seize somebody else's place'.

Time passed and the twins grew very different in personality as well as looks. Jacob was quiet and thoughtful. He loved spending time at home with his mother in the kitchen, and they became very close. However, Esau was strong and brave. He loved roaming around outside and he

became an excellent hunter. Esau was his father's favourite son.

Whenever Jacob saw his father and brother together, talking and laughing in easy companionship, he couldn't help but wish that he was loved best by Isaac instead. To make matters worse, because Esau had been born before Jacob, the law said that Esau was to be given all of their father's wealth when he died. This was called his birthright. Jacob knew that he was cleverer than Esau and better suited to running his father's business. He couldn't stand to think that it was Esau's birthright to take it over eventually.

One day, Jacob was in the kitchen cooking a delicious bean stew when Esau

arrived back from a hunt.
"Ooooh, what's that? I'm
STARVING!" he exclaimed,
bending over the cooking pot
and breathing in the aroma.
"Can I have some now?"
he begged.

Jacob's eyes glinted with
an idea. "I'll give you some
stew," he replied, "if you
promise to give me all your
rights as the firstborn son."

"Done!" agreed Esau. All he
could think about was his rumbling
stomach, burning with hunger. "If I don't
get anything to eat within the next five
minutes I'll fall over and die anyway, so

what use would my birthright be then?" he joked.

But Jacob was quite serious. "Say you solemnly swear," he insisted.

"I solemnly swear," promised Esau. "Now come on, give me that stew!"

Jacob ladled some stew into a bowl and gave Esau some soft, baked bread, and both twins sat back, highly pleased.

Twenty years passed and Isaac was an old, blind man who knew he didn't have long to live. One of Isaac's last wishes was for Esau to go hunting for meat for his favourite meal. Afterwards, Isaac was going to give his eldest son the blessing that officially gave him his birthright. Esau set off with his bow and arrows at once.

But Rebecca had overheard. All at once, a plan came to her to trick her husband into giving her favourite son Jacob the blessing instead! First, she quickly cooked the meal her husband had asked for. Then she hurriedly dressed Jacob in Esau's clothes so he would smell like his brother, and wrapped goatskin round his arms and neck so he would feel hairy like his brother too.

"But- But- " protested Jacob.

"I'll take the blame," Rebecca reassured her son, and sent him in with the food to see his father.

The trick worked perfectly. Isaac was at first suspicious because his tasty dinner had arrived so quickly, but Jacob said that God had helped him in his hunting. Jacob copied

Esau's voice and, of course, he smelled and felt like his brother too. Isaac was fooled into thinking that Jacob was Esau, and gave him the all-important birthright blessing.

When Esau arrived back from the hunt and went to his father, they both quickly realized they had been tricked. How they wept with frustration and regret. But it was too late, the old man could not take back his blessing.

Later, in private, Esau began to feel angry. "I'll wait until father dies," he swore to himself, "but no longer than that. Then I shall have my revenge on Jacob."

Genesis chapters 25 to 28

Jacob's Dream

Jacob had to leave home after angering his father. While wandering in the desert he had a strange dream in which God repeated a promise that Jacob would one day be the father of a great nation.

Jacob had won his twin brother Esau's birthright, but his joy soon melted into shame and regret. His old, blind father was so bitterly disappointed that he could hardly talk to Jacob, and Esau couldn't stand the sight of him either. It was only because Esau didn't want to upset his father even further that he hadn't already had a fight with his smaller, weaker twin brother. Only Jacob's mother still loved him – and now he was about to lose her too. Rebecca was so worried about what Esau would do to her favourite son once Isaac died, that she told Jacob he had no choice but to leave. "You must go far away, well out of Esau's reach," Rebecca urged. "Hurry to my brother, your Uncle Laban, in the city of Haran. You'll be safe there. We'll just have to hope that your brother cools down and forgives you, so you can come back."

So Jacob left his home and his family in disgrace, with no one for company and no possessions for comfort. He set off for Haran through the desert, wondering why he had

done what he had done. At the end of the
first lonely day's travelling, Jacob came
across a rocky, sheltered spot where he
could camp for the night. Weary and
miserable, Jacob found a flattish, smooth
stone that would have to do as a pillow and
laid down to try to get some rest.

Alone in the desert, hungry, cold and
worried about wild animals, Jacob did not
sleep well. He tossed and turned for hours,
and when he did eventually fall asleep he
had a very strange dream.

Jacob dreamt that a blinding light
suddenly burst from the dark night sky. He
shielded his eyes and blinked until he got
used to the glare and could open them
properly. Then Jacob saw that the light

shone in a steady, sloping beam down to
the ground. People in bright, shimmering
clothes were gliding up and down. With a
shock, Jacob realized that he was looking at
a staircase from Heaven to Earth and that
the people were angels. Suddenly he felt
God Himself standing beside him. "Yes,
I am the Lord," said God. "And as I
promised your grandfather Abraham
and your father Isaac, I am going to
give the land on which you are lying to
you and your family. You will have as
many descendants as there are specks of
dust on the ground. Now remember, you
will never be alone. I will always be with
you. I will look after you, and wherever
you go, I will make sure that one day you

return safely back home."

Then the staircase and the
angels faded away and the
voice was gone. Jacob woke up,
lying stiff and cold on his own
in the desert. But he knew
God had been there and was
watching over him.

Genesis chapters 27, 28

Jacob Makes Amends

Jacob finally decided that he should apologize to his brother Esau, and on his way home he had another strange experience. All night he wrestled with a mysterious stranger, someone he was sure he had met before.

Jacob reached Haran and went to work on his Uncle Laban's farm. He vowed to work for his uncle for fourteen years, and he married Laban's daughters Rachel and Leah.

Jacob was a very skilled farmer. With him in charge, his Uncle Laban's flocks and

herds grew several times bigger and the
sheep, cattle and goats were fatter and finer
than ever. Jacob stayed longer than the
fourteen years he had promised, and built
up stocks of animals for himself. Eventually
he became even wealthier than his uncle.

Finally Jacob decided that enough was
enough, he wanted to return home. He told
his wives and they ordered the servants to
pack everything up and prepare the
animals. They all set off in a long train
across the countryside.

As Jacob drew closer to Canaan, he
became more and more worried. After all,
when he left, his brother Esau had been
determined to kill him! Jacob sent
messengers galloping ahead, to tell Esau

that he was coming and that he wanted to make amends. But he was worried to see his messengers returning so soon. "Sir," they panted, "your brother is heading this way with a force of four hundred men!"

"Then Esau must have made up his mind to attack me," Jacob told himself in deep dismay. He ordered his herders to count out two hundred and twenty goats, two hundred and twenty sheep, thirty camels and their young, forty cows, ten bulls and thirty donkeys. "Keep all the animals separate," Jacob instructed the herders. "Drive every group forward an hour apart and when you each reach Esau, tell him that the animals are a present from me." Jacob thought that perhaps by the time he sees Esau, he may have forgiven him.

That evening Jacob camped on his own. He knew it might be his last night. As darkness drew in, he lay awake thinking everything over. Suddenly, from nowhere, a man jumped on Jacob and began to attack him. Stunned, Jacob fought for his life, but the stranger didn't give in. They wrestled for hours, until finally – CRACK! Jacob collapsed in agony as one of the stranger's blows put his hip out of joint.

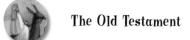

"I am the Lord," the stranger announced, and Jacob was stunned to realize that it was God Himself. "You have done well," God continued. "You have won your struggles with others and now I say you have won your struggle with me too. I want you to change your name. From now on, everyone should call you Israel."

The sun rose and God was gone. Jacob hobbled away to rejoin his family.

It wasn't long before Esau and his four hundred men arrived in a cloud of dust. Jacob told his family to stay well back and limped forward all alone to face his brother. Esau jumped off his horse and ran forwards, and Jacob sank to his knees before his brother, bowing low in the dirt. But Esau hurried to help him up, throwing his arms around Jacob, kissing him, and both the brothers began to weep.

"Welcome, my long-lost brother," Esau sobbed. "Welcome to you and your family."

And Jacob was overjoyed to be home at last.

Genesis chapters 30 to 33

Joseph the Dreamer

Jacob became wealthy and had a large family of twelve sons and one daughter. Joseph was Jacob's favourite son and this made his other brothers jealous. One day, Jacob gave Joseph a beautiful coat and this made his brothers madder than ever.

Jacob was one of the wealthiest men in Canaan. He had vast herds of cattle, sheep, goats, camels and donkeys, and he owned many tents, filled with possessions. However the thing he held most dear was Joseph, his eleventh son, the first of two sons by Jacob's true love, Rachel. The couple

had waited for many years before God sent them a child. So long that Jacob had ten sons by three other wives by then. So Joseph was very special.

Unfortunately, Jacob made it obvious that Joseph was his favourite. He sometimes kept Joseph at home with him while his other sons went into the fields on farming duties. Of course this made Jacob's other sons resentful of their brother. Even more so when Joseph turned seventeen. Jacob had an expensive coat made for him. It was a

beautiful, long coat with big sleeves, richly sewn with many different colours. It drove Jacob's other sons wild with jealousy.

The situation went from bad to worse when Joseph began to have strange dreams.

"Guess what?" he asked his brothers one morning. "Last night, I dreamt that we were in the fields at harvest time tying the wheat into sheaves, when my sheaf stood up straight. Then your sheaves gathered around it and bowed to mine!"

"Who do you think you are?" spat one of the brothers.

"Do you see yourself as better than us?" growled another.

"Do you think you're going to be a king and rule over us?" scowled a third.

A little while later, Joseph had another odd dream and again made the mistake of telling his brothers about it.

"I dreamt last night that I saw the sun, the moon and eleven stars all bowing down to me." The brothers knew that Joseph meant that their father, mother and the eleven of them were like his servants. How furious they were!

One day, when Jacob had kept Joseph at home with him and sent his other sons out to work, he decided to send Joseph to check on them. Out in the hot fields, the tired, thirsty brothers saw him coming, fresh from home, all dressed up in his fancy coat and they had a terrible idea.

"Here comes the dreamer!" one of them

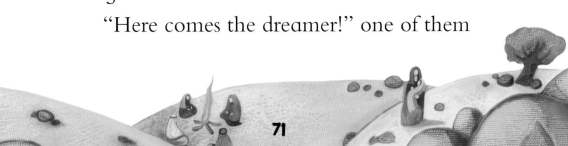

laughed. "I wish we could get rid of him once and for all."

"Well, this is our chance," another noticed.

"There's no one around, it's the perfect opportunity!" a third brother agreed.

"Let's kill him and throw the body into that pit over there," another brother urged.

"We could tell our father that he was attacked by wild animals!" one lad suggested.

"Stop it!" cried the eldest brother, Reuben, horrified. "We can't kill Joseph! Do you really want his blood on your hands?" he pointed out. "If you must, throw him into that old, dry well over there and leave him — but don't murder him!" (Little

did the brothers know that
once they'd all gone home,
Reuben intended to sneak
off back to the well and
rescue Joseph).

And that's what the
brothers did. They fell
on Joseph, ripping off
his special coat, and
then lowered him into
the dried-up well,
taking away the rope.

Pleased with
themselves, the brothers

ignored Joseph's cries for help, and sat down
to eat – all except Reuben. He didn't feel
like joining them. He stomped off on his

own to see to the animals in the furthest pastures.

While Reuben was gone, a camel train of spice traders came passing by on their way to Egypt. One of the brothers, Judah, had another awful idea. "Reuben was right. We shouldn't harm Joseph – he is our flesh and blood, after all," he announced, with a glint in his eye. "I have a better plan – we'll sell him instead. I'm sure the traders will pay a good price for a slave."

By the time Reuben returned, Judah and the brothers had accepted twenty pieces of silver from the traders and Joseph was gone.

"What have you done?" Reuben cried. "Shame on you, Judah. Shame on you all! Now what are you going to tell Father?"

In desperation, the brothers came up with a final part to their wicked plan. They killed a young goat, dipped Joseph's torn coat in its blood and took it home to show their father. "Joseph was killed and eaten by wild animals," they explained to Jacob.

The old man collapsed in sorrow, weeping and mourning for his beloved Joseph. "I will grieve for my son until the day I die," he sobbed.

Genesis chapter 37

A Slave in Egypt

After being thrown down a well and then sold by his brothers to passing traders, Joseph was taken to Egypt where he was sold as a slave. Then Joseph found himself unfairly imprisoned, but God stayed with him and looked after him.

Sold by his family, marched by strangers all the way to a foreign land, and then traded in the market place as a slave — Joseph was exhausted and terrified. Yet his strong character must have shone through because the man who bought Joseph trusted him to work in his house, not in his fields or as a labourer. The man was very important and wealthy. His name was Potiphar and he was captain of the soldiers who guarded Pharaoh, the king of Egypt. God stayed with Joseph all the time and cheered him up, helping him do his duties well. Potiphar was so pleased that he kept promoting Joseph. After a while, Joseph was running Potiphar's whole household.

Now Joseph was not only hard-working and trustworthy, he was also quite handsome. So much so that Potiphar's wife fell in love with him. Each day, she seized every opportunity behind her husband's back to flirt with Joseph, trying to tempt him into having an affair. Joseph was loyal to Potiphar and kept turning her down. But

Potiphar's wife was determined to get what she wanted. One day, she lay in wait for Joseph and grabbed him by his cloak. Joseph had to wriggle out of it in order to escape her clutches and run off! Then the scorned woman saw a way to get her own back. She put on a show of being deeply upset and accused Joseph of having forced his way into her bedroom. She said that when she screamed out, he had ran away, leaving only his cloak behind.

Of course, Potiphar was furious. He had Joseph flung into prison.

Joseph could have wept and wailed. He could have despaired and died, but God stayed with him and lifted his spirits. The jailer was fond of the reliable, capable young man and began giving him special jobs. Soon, he put Joseph in charge of all the other prisoners.

Two of the prisoners in Joseph's care were Pharaoh's butler and baker. One morning, Joseph found them looking anxious because they had both had strange dreams that they couldn't understand.

"Tell me about them," Joseph urged. "Maybe God will explain to me what they're about."

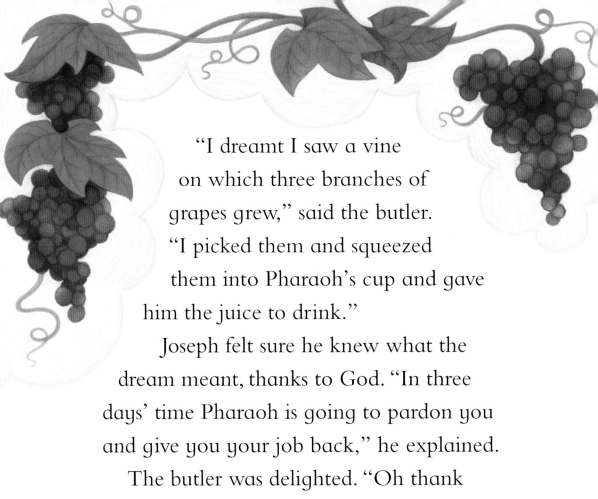

"I dreamt I saw a vine on which three branches of grapes grew," said the butler. "I picked them and squeezed them into Pharaoh's cup and gave him the juice to drink."

Joseph felt sure he knew what the dream meant, thanks to God. "In three days' time Pharaoh is going to pardon you and give you your job back," he explained.

The butler was delighted. "Oh thank you! Thank you so much!" he cried.

"My friend," Joseph said, "just promise me that when you're released, you won't forget about me. Please tell Pharaoh about me and beg him to release me, for I don't deserve to be in here!"

"Well, what about my dream?" asked the baker excitedly. "I dreamt I was carrying three baskets of white bread on my head, and the birds were eating the bread out of the top basket."

Joseph's face fell as the meaning came to him. "I hate to tell you this," he said sadly, "but in three days' time, Pharaoh is going to hang you."

The dreams came true. In three days' time the baker was put to death, while the butler was released and set back to work for Pharaoh. He was so joyful that any thoughts of Joseph went out of his head. Joseph remained in prison, quite forgotten.

Genesis chapters 39, 40

The Ruler of Egypt

Suddenly, Joseph's life changed for the better. His amazing gift for explaining the meaning of dreams saved him. One minute he was in prison and the next he had become a rich and powerful ruler in Egypt.

One morning, there was a commotion in the royal palace of Egypt. Pharaoh had awoken deeply troubled. He had had two strange dreams, which he was sure meant something but he had no idea what.

In the first dream, Pharaoh had been standing by the River Nile. Seven fat cows

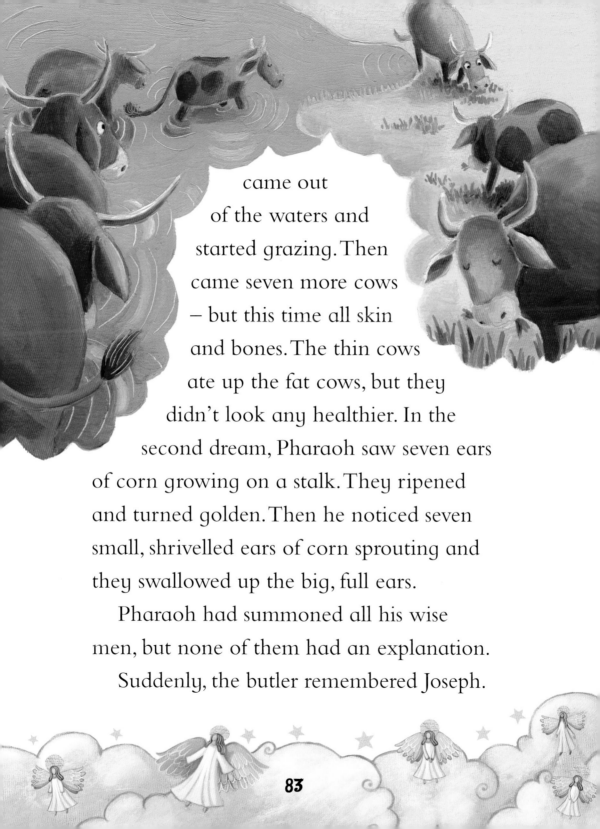

came out
of the waters and
started grazing. Then
came seven more cows
– but this time all skin
and bones. The thin cows
ate up the fat cows, but they
didn't look any healthier. In the
second dream, Pharaoh saw seven ears
of corn growing on a stalk. They ripened
and turned golden. Then he noticed seven
small, shrivelled ears of corn sprouting and
they swallowed up the big, full ears.

Pharaoh had summoned all his wise
men, but none of them had an explanation.
Suddenly, the butler remembered Joseph.

Two years had passed and he wasn't even sure if Joseph was still alive. But now he told Pharaoh all about the amazing young Israelite man locked in the dungeon.

Pharaoh sent for him at once. Joseph was hauled out of prison and brought into the magnificent courtroom of the great king of Egypt. Then Pharaoh described his dreams and Joseph felt God give him the interpretation.

"Both dreams mean the same," Joseph announced to the anxiously waiting king. "For the next seven years, Egypt will have excellent harvests. But during the following seven years the crops will fail and there will be a terrible famine. Here's what God says to do. Hire a minister with officials under him to take charge of your kingdom. For the next seven years, they should collect one-fifth of all the grain that is grown and store it away in warehouses. During the seven years of famine, you can share out the grain so your people don't starve."

"Really?" said Pharaoh. "Is that what your God thinks?" He thought for a while and everyone in the courtroom held their breath to see whether the king was pleased.

Pharaoh descended from his gleaming throne and approached Joseph. He took a huge gold ring off his finger and gave it to the former prisoner. "You will be the minister," he ordered. "I can't think of anyone better. You start straight away."

Genesis chapter 41

The Baby in the Basket

This story is about baby Moses and how his brave mother and sister made a plan to save his life. Little did they know that he would grow up to save his people, the Israleites.

The seven-year famine happened just as Pharaoh's dream predicted, and in this time Joseph made amends with his brothers. His family came to live with him in Egypt, where his father Jacob lived out the rest of his years, and Joseph's brothers went on to have many children, grandchildren and

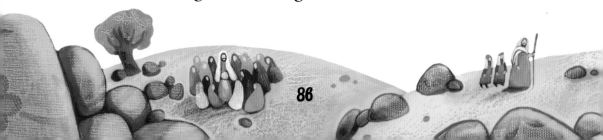

great-grandchildren.

They did well in farming and business and became wealthy and powerful. As time passed, the Egyptians began calling them Israelites after the special name God had given to Jacob. Years went by and the number of Israelites grew, and different pharaohs came and went. After four hundred years, one king became particularly worried because there were so many Israelites. He told his advisors, "I am worried that if there was ever a war, the Israelites might turn against us and join with our enemies to defeat Egypt. We must find a way to stop their numbers growing further and to make them less powerful."

Pharaoh decided on drastic action – he

sent his soldiers to seize the Israelites and turn them into slaves. He set them to work, labouring on building sites and in the fields.

But still the number of Israelites increased, and families spread further throughout Egypt. Furious, Pharaoh came up with an even more wicked plan. He ordered his soldiers to search out every newborn Israelite boy and kill them all!

Of course, many desperate families tried to hide their beloved babies. One woman, who already had a daughter, Miriam, and a son, Aaron, kept her newborn boy hidden for three months. But as time went on, he became bigger and noisier and harder to conceal. In the end, the desperate woman took a reed basket and covered it with tar

so it was watertight. She gently laid her
baby in it and took it down to the River
Nile, setting it in the thick, tall grasses at the
water's edge so it wouldn't float away. She
told Miriam to stay a little way off to see
that the baby was alright.

It wasn't long before the little girl saw a
procession making its way down to the
river. Her eyes opened wide at the sight of a
young woman in magnificent robes, jewels
and makeup, accompanied by many
servants and slaves. It was the princess,
coming to bathe! The little girl watched,
hardly daring to breathe, as the princess
caught sight of the basket in the rushes and
sent a servant to bring it to her. As soon as
the princess saw the baby boy inside, she

realized that he must be an Israelite. As she lifted the baby up her heart melted with pity and she decided to take the baby home.

Bravely, Miriam approached the princess. "Would you like me to find an Israelite nurse to look after him, Your Highness?" she suggested nervously.

The princess was pleased, and the little girl dashed home and fetched her mother!

The little boy was at first cared for by his mother, then given the education of an Egyptian prince. The princess loved him so much that she adopted him as her own son. She called him Moses, which means 'to draw out', because she had rescued him by having him drawn out of the water.

Exodus chapters 1, 2

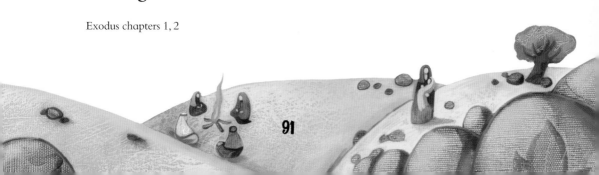

The Burning Bush

Something amazing happened to Moses. Alone in the desert, he was given a message from God that he was to save his people from slavery.

Moses was brought up as Egyptian royalty, but he knew that he was an Israelite by birth. As he grew up, he found it unbearable that he was living a rich, comfortable life of freedom, while other Israelites suffered as Egyptian slaves. One day, when he was a young man, he saw an

Egyptian guard savagely hitting an Israelite
man, and something inside him snapped.
Moses beat the guard off, leaving him lying
dead at his feet. News of his crime quickly
spread. Moses knew that even the princess
would not be able to save him from a
terrible punishment, perhaps even death. He
had no choice but to run away.

Moses fled to a country called Midian
and settled into the quiet life of a shepherd.
He looked after the flocks belonging to a
village priest named Jethro, and he married
his daughter, Zipporah. Years came and
went and Moses' former life as an Egyptian
royal seemed like a dream.

One day, Moses was out with his sheep
when he came upon a very strange sight.

A bush was on fire, but the leaves
and branches of the bush
weren't burning away.
While Moses marvelled,
a voice suddenly
boomed, "Moses,
come no closer to
this holy place! I
am God – the God
of your fathers,
Abraham, Isaac
and Jacob."

Moses fell to the ground,
covering his face in terror.

"I have seen how my people, the
Israelites, suffer in Egypt," echoed the voice.
"But I will free them from slavery and

return them to Canaan, a land of plenty that I promised would be their own. I want you to return to Egypt and rescue my people. Convince them to follow you and demand Pharaoh to release them."

Moses was shocked. "No one will believe that my orders are from you, Lord," he protested.

God gave Moses three magic signs so that he could prove it. Firstly, if Moses threw his shepherd's staff onto the ground, it turned into a snake! As soon as he picked it up again, it turned back into wood. Secondly, if Moses thrust his hand into his robe, it came out covered with scales and sores of the disease leprosy! When he put it back again, it was healed and healthy.

Lastly, God told Moses that if he poured some water from the River Nile onto the ground, it would turn into blood!

Moses was stunned, but even so, he was still unsure. "How can I be a leader, Lord?" he argued. "I don't even like talking in public. I go red and can't get the words out. Isn't there someone else you can send?"

"I have already told your brother Aaron to come and find you – he can do the talking," insisted God.

Moses hurried home and explained to his wife and his father-in-law what he had been ordered to do. To Moses' great surprise, Jethro believed him. God reassured Moses that it was safe for him to return to Egypt as a new pharaoh had come to the throne.

So he and his wife packed up and set off through the countryside.

As they neared Egypt, Aaron came out to meet them, just as God had promised. The long-lost brothers hurried to see the Israelite elders straight away. While Aaron explained that God had told Moses to lead the Israelites out of slavery, Moses proved that his message was from God by demonstrating the three magic signs in front of everyone. How the Israelites gasped! They believed Moses and sent up prayers of thanks that God had sent them help.

Exodus chapters 2 to 4

The Nine Plagues of Egypt

Pharaoh was determined to keep the Israelites as his slaves and Moses was determined that they would be set free. God sent nine terrible plagues to devastate the country, but was this enough to make Pharaoh change his mind and set the Israelites free?

As God had ordered, Moses and Aaron requested an audience with Pharaoh. They were summoned to appear in his magnificent courtroom, in front of all his guards, advisors and magicians. "We have come at God's command to ask that you set the people of Israel free!" the brothers dared to tell Pharaoh.

But Pharaoh just laughed and waved for Moses and Aaron to be taken away. Then he set the Israelites even tougher tasks to do, making their lives even harder.

"I've made the situation worse!" Moses told God, but God insisted that he try again.

So once more Moses and Aaron went to see Pharaoh. This time Aaron threw down Moses' staff, which turned into a snake, wriggling on the floor. Pharaoh signalled to his magicians and they too threw their staffs onto the floor, which also turned into slithering snakes. Pharaoh didn't even care when Aaron's snake swallowed up all of the

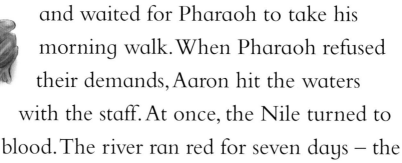

magicians' snakes. "Audience over," he announced coldly.

Moses despaired, but God told him what to do. Early the next day, Moses and Aaron went down to the River Nile and waited for Pharaoh to take his morning walk. When Pharaoh refused their demands, Aaron hit the waters with the staff. At once, the Nile turned to blood. The river ran red for seven days – the fish died and there was no water to drink.

Yet the cold-hearted king was unmoved. Then Moses signalled Aaron to stretch the staff over the Nile, and millions of frogs came hopping out of every river, stream and pond in Egypt. Everywhere anyone looked there were frogs… the

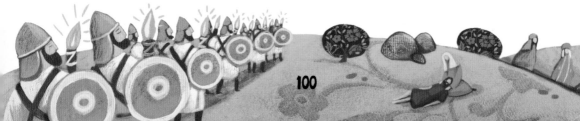

people couldn't move for frogs!

Then Pharaoh sent for Moses. "Tell your god to make this stop and I will let your people go."

Immediately, there were so many dead frogs that the Egyptians had to pile them into huge, stinking heaps.

Pharaoh went back on his word.

So God ordered Moses to tell Aaron to hit the ground with the staff. Billions of lice swarmed out of the ground. Soon, everything that had been covered in slimy frogs was itching with lice.

But Pharaoh's heart was as hard as stone.

So God sent vast clouds of flies humming into Egypt. They darkened the skies and blanketed the ground. But not one fly

entered the house of an Israelite.

Then Pharaoh summoned Moses. "I will do as you ask," he announced, "if your god rids us of these flies!"

Once again, as soon as the flies were gone, Pharaoh simply broke his promise.

So God sent a dreadful disease which wiped out every horse, camel, ox, goat and sheep in the land – except for those belonging to the Israelites.

Still, Pharaoh would not give in.

Then God told Moses and Aaron to take a handful of ashes and throw it up into the air. As the wind blew the ashes across Egypt, a sickness spread, which caused boils to break out over every person and remaining animal – unless they were Israelite.

It just made Pharaoh more determined.

So God told Moses to stretch his staff up to the heavens… Thunder crashed, lighting flashed and hail fell from the skies, flattening trees and plants. Everywhere except in the fields of the Israelites.

At last Pharaoh called Moses again. "Enough!" he spat. "Make it stop and I will do what you ask." Moses prayed and the storm calmed. "I lied," announced Pharaoh triumphantly. He turned and strode away.

The very next day, a strange wind blew across Egypt, thick with locusts. Within a few hours the insects had eaten every leaf, every ear of corn, every fruit on the trees.

"Aaaaaaargh!" howled Pharaoh. "Alright, the Israelites can go." The wind

changed direction and the locusts were blown into the Red Sea and drowned.

But still, Pharaoh did not keep his promise. So God told Moses to stretch out his hand and Egypt was swamped in darkness for three days. As his people stumbled around and the country ground to a halt, Pharaoh summoned Moses. "The Israelites may go. This time I will not go back on my word," he spat. "As long as they leave all their animals."

Moses listened to God.

"No," he replied. Pharaoh was furious.

"Then get out," roared the cruel king. "Your people will be my slaves forever. If I ever lay eyes on you again, you will die!"

Exodus chapters 5 to 10

The First Passover

The events of the first Passover are celebrated by Jewish people every year. They share special food, including unleavened bread and roasted lamb. This reminds them of the last meal eaten by the Israelites before God saved them from slavery in Egypt.

God spoke to Moses and said, "I am going to send one last plague upon Egypt, so terrible that Pharaoh will be glad to let the Israelites go. At midnight, every firstborn child in Egypt shall die. From the firstborn of Pharaoh to the firstborn of the lowliest servant to the firstborn of every animal. No one shall escape – unless they are an Israelite. Here's what they have to do to be spared. Every family must cook a lamb and smear their doorposts with the blood. Then I shall know which houses are Israelite homes. Forever after, this day will be called Passover and celebrated as the first day of the year. By my passing over the land tonight, my people will be set free – the beginning of a new era."

Next morning, nothing could be heard in Egypt except for wailing and screaming as people discovered their loved ones were dead. People and animals had breathed their last in every household across the land – except for the homes of the Israelites.

Once again Moses and Aaron found

themselves before Pharaoh, who was weeping over his own dead firstborn son. "Take your people and go!" he whispered. "Be gone, and never darken my lands again."

All over Pharaoh's country, the doomed Egyptians were so desperate to be rid of the Israelites that they offered them gold, silver and jewels to leave right away.

And that is how over six hundred thousand men, women and children came to gather to walk out of Egypt. After over four hundred years of captivity, the Israelites were heading home.

Exodus chapters 11, 12

Escape Across the Red Sea

The Israelites' escaped from Egypt. God showed that He was all powerful and protected them. Moses proved that he was a great leader who could bring the Israelites to the land that God had promised to them.

God Himself guided the Israelites as they travelled out of Egypt and into the wilderness beyond. By day He appeared as a column of cloud and by night, as a column of fire, so they could follow Him.

The Israelites had reached the sands of the Red Sea when they noticed a massive

cloud of dust behind them in the distance, rushing towards them at great speed.

It was the Egyptian army! The minute that Pharaoh had ordered the Israelites to leave, he regretted his decision. In a whirlwind of hatred, he called for his best armour and ordered six hundred of his finest charioteers to make ready to chase after his former slaves.

The Israelites were terrified and turned on Moses. "Did you lead us out of captivity only to meet our deaths in the desert?" they cried.

"Don't be afraid," Moses told the Israelites. "The Lord will protect you, wait and see." And God spoke to Moses, telling him what to do.

With the Egyptian army thundering ever closer, Moses urged the Israelites forward – straight towards the Red Sea. Then the column of cloud blew over Pharaoh and his charioteers, smothering them so they couldn't see their way ahead. While the bewildered, frustrated Egyptians were forced to slow their pace, Moses reached the foaming seashore and stretched out his hand towards the ocean.

An immense wind blew up, nearly sweeping the Israelites off their feet. It howled and hurled, and with great gusts this way and that it split the waves. The wind drove the waters to the right and left, higher and higher, until they rolled back leaving a wide pathway of seabed in between. Then

bravely and boldly,
Moses strode down the sand, leading the
Israelites between the towering walls of
water on either side.

Then came the Egyptian army,
galloping forwards. How petrified they were
when they saw the waters of the Red Sea

divided in front of them. Yet they plunged into the passage as the last of the Israelites reached the sandy shore on the other side.

As Pharaoh and his charioteers sped ever closer to the Israelites, Moses stretched out his hand once more. Then the towering walls of water teetered, toppled and crashed down. The Red Sea closed over the Egyptians, drowning each and every one, and the Israelites were truly free at last.

Exodus chapters 13, 14

The Ten Commandments

One day, God called Moses to the top of a mountain. There He gave Moses ten special rules that He wanted people to live by. But when Moses returned to the Israelites, things had started to go badly wrong.

The Israelites trusted Moses and followed him uncomplainingly into the hot, rocky desert. After three months, the Israelites arrived at the foot of the holy mountain of Sinai. Moses announced they would camp there a while. He told them that they should make ready with prayers and rituals because in three days' time God was going to speak to all of them.

Sure enough, on the morning of the third day, black storm clouds gathered around the peak of the mountain. Thunder rumbled and lightning split the skies. Then the earth shook, and the mountain began to spew out flames and smoke as if it were an enormous furnace. A sound like a giant trumpet blared out through the air, calling the terrified Israelites to assemble at the foot of the mountain. Then Moses slowly climbed up and up towards the smoking, fiery mountain-top and disappeared from view into the clouds.

For a long time after he had gone, thunder continued to echo around the slopes and many Israelites thought it was the voice of God talking to their leader. When the noise had at last died away, Moses came back down the mountain and announced that God had given him ten important rules of behaviour:

1.   *You should not worship any other god but me.*

2.   *You should not make a statue or a picture to worship.*

3.   *You should only use my name respectfully.*

4.   *You should keep the seventh day, or Sabbath, of every week as a holy day of rest.*

5.   *You should always be respectful to your parents.*

6.   *You should never commit murder.*

7.   *You should never be unfaithful to your partner.*

8.   *You should not steal.*

9.   *You should not lie.*

10. *You should not envy the things that other people have.*

Moses wrote the Ten Commandments down, and lots of lesser rules too. The very next day he built an altar at the foot of the mountain and asked the Israelites to vow to obey the rules. Then Moses made a sacrifice to seal their solemn promise.

Yet God still had more that He wanted the Israelites to learn, so He summoned Moses up the mountain once more, where they could talk on their own together. The Israelites watched as their leader climbed up the mountain one more time and disappeared alone into the dark clouds.

The Israelites watched and waited for Moses to return… watched and waited for seven long weeks, but there was no sign of their leader. Worried and confused, they came to the conclusion that God had abandoned them and Moses would never return.

"Make something for us to worship," they begged Aaron. "We need something we can see and touch." Thousands of men and women brought Aaron their gold jewellery. He melted it down and made an enormous statue of a calf, one of the animals that was sometimes sacrificed to God. To please the people and keep them under control, Aaron even built the calf an enormous altar and declared there would be a festival in its honour.

The people were delighted. At last they

had a straightforward god. One that wasn't invisible and didn't speak to them in thunder, giving them complicated lists of things they should and shouldn't do. Immediately, the Israelites began praying to the calf and offering it sacrifices, and singing and dancing around it.

As they did so, Moses came clambering down the mountainside at last. He held two huge stone tablets on which God Himself had written out the ten most important commandments so that no one could forget them or get them wrong.

Moses knew already about how the Israelites were worshipping the golden calf because God had told him while they were up the mountain. God had been full of fury and so was Moses. Enraged at the sight that met his eyes as he approached the camp, he threw the stone tablets to the ground and they shattered into pieces. Then he hurled the golden calf into the flames of one of the sacrificial fires.

"Aaron, what did everyone do to you that you allowed this to happen?" Moses spat with disgust at his brother. Then he called for anyone who was on God's side to go and stand next to him. Only the men of the tribe of Levi took up places next to

Moses. On God's orders, he told each of them to grab a sword and put to death everyone who stood in their way as punishment for their sins.

Over three thousand Israelites were killed that night. The next day, Moses went back up the mountain to pray to God for forgiveness for the wickedness of His Chosen People.

Exodus chapters 19 to 24, 32

Joshua and the Battle of Jericho

Although Moses did not live to enter the Promised Land, he trained Joshua to take over as leader of the Israelites. Joshua's first job was to conquer the walled city of Jericho. His tactics were very unusual – and very noisy!

Moses returned from Mount Sinai with two new stone tablets on which God had again written the Ten Commandments. On God's command the Israelites built an ornate chest for the tablets to be kept in, which was called the Ark of the Covenant.

After many more years wandering in the

wilderness, at last God thought the Israelites had earned the right to enter Canaan, the land He had long ago promised Abraham would be theirs.

The Israelites had to fight against the tribes in the lands around Canaan for many years. So many that Moses never got to enter the country that God had chosen for his people. When the time drew near that Moses realized he was going to die, he climbed up to a mountain-top and God showed him the Promised Land spread out far below. And so Moses died comforted, and a warrior called Joshua took over as ruler of the Israelites.

Then God told Joshua to be brave and bold. It was finally time to cross the River

Jordan, which was all that remained to keep the Israelites from entering the Promised Land. So Joshua told the people to prepare to fight. Meanwhile, he sent spies across the river into the city of Jericho to find out what they were up against. The spies were nearly discovered by the king's soldiers, but a woman called Rahab helped the spies escape. In return, she asked for their promise that Joshua's army would not harm her family when they invaded. Joshua learnt about the city and the strength of its mighty walls. He drew up battle plans and prayed to God for help.

Then came the day when Joshua gathered the Israelites on the banks of the River Jordan and commanded everyone to listen carefully. "As soon as the priests carrying the Ark of the Covenant at the front step into the river, the waters will stop flowing. Then we will all be able to cross."

To the Israelites' astonishment and joy, it happened exactly as their leader had said. Finally, Joshua's army of forty thousand men stood on a plain in the Promised Land.

The walls of the mighty city were thick and high, and the city gates were barred against them. But Joshua listened to God, who told him exactly what to do.

Every day for six days, the Israelite army marched around the city walls. Behind the soldiers, priests with trumpets made of rams' horns carried the Ark of the Covenant.

For Jericho's people it was a terrifying and mysterious display of strength. What are the Israelites up to they wondered? Does that Ark really have magical powers? And why are they marching in that eerie silence? When will they attack?

Then on the seventh day the silence ceased and an almighty noise began. Joshua gave the order for the priests to blow their horns for all they were worth as the army marched six times around the city walls. As they began a seventh circuit, Joshua signalled for his soldiers to shout as loud as they could. Then such a roaring joined the blaring of the horns that the walls of Jericho trembled, shook… and then with a fearful rumble, collapsed to the ground.

Joshua's army entered the city and killed every man, woman and child they found there – all except for Rahab and her household, as she had been promised.

Deuteronomy chapter 34; Joshua chapters 1 to 6

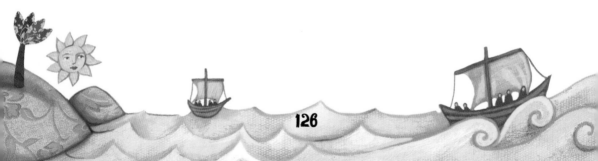

Samson
the Strong

Samson was sent by God to fight against the Philistines who ruled over the Israelites, but he fell in love with a Philistine girl. Samson was tempted by the beautiful Delilah to reveal his one great secret – but with terrible consequences.

The Israelites suffered for many years at the hands of a people called the Philistines. However one day an angel appeared to an Israelite couple and gave a prediction: "You will have a son who will fight for Israel against the Philistines. You must raise him to worship God according to

the strict rules of the Nazirite sect, and one of these rules is that you must be careful never to cut his hair."

The couple were overjoyed when they did indeed have a baby boy. They called their little son Samson, but he didn't stay little for long. God ensured that Samson grew up to be tall and strong. He was so strong that once, when he was attacked by a lion, he killed it with his bare hands!

To his parents' immense dismay, Samson fell in love with a Philistine girl, and he insisted on marrying her. At the wedding, Samson set his bride's guests a difficult riddle. They tried for three days to work it out but couldn't come up with the answer. In the end, the guests pestered the bride to find out, and she persuaded Samson to tell her so she could tell them. Samson realized what his new wife had done. In a temper, he killed thirty Philistines, and stormed off back home. By the time he calmed down and returned to reclaim his bride, she had married someone else! Samson was so furious that he burned the Philistine harvest fields. When the Philistines found out why, they burned down the house of his

former bride in turn. With this, Samson's
rage knew no bounds and he single-
handedly killed many more Philistines
before he returned home.

From then on Samson was the
Philistines' sworn enemy. They demanded
that some Israelites from the tribe of Judah
hand him over, or face the consequences.
The men explained the situation to Samson,
and Samson agreed to be bound and taken
to his enemies. But once surrounded, he
burst out of his ropes and attacked the
Philistines, grabbing a nearby bone to use
as a weapon. He left them all for dead
before escaping.

Eventually the giant man became the
leader of all Israel. He ruled for twenty

years, but the Philistines never gave up trying to capture him. Once, they waited until Samson was in the city of Gaza. They knew he would leave the next morning and planned to attack him by surprise at the city gates. But when they went there at dawn, they found that Samson had outsmarted them. He had left in the middle of the night, uprooting the massive, locked gates and carrying them off!

The Philistines saw yet another chance to take revenge on Samson when he fell in love with a woman called Delilah. Philistine chiefs visited Delilah and promised to pay her five thousand and five hundred pieces of silver if she handed him over to them. So each time Samson visited Delilah, she tested

his great strength and tried to persuade him to tell her the secret of it. Eventually, Samson gave in. "My parents promised God that I would never have my hair cut," he explained. "If I cut my hair, I lose God's protection and my strength will be gone."

Delilah's eyes lit up. At last, she knew! Next time Samson came to visit, she gave him wine and gradually he fell asleep.

Then she cut off his hair and called the Philistines. It wasn't enough for Samson's enemies to bind him in chains, they blinded him too. Then they threw him in prison and set him to work as a slave.

Around a year passed, and the day came when the Philistines held a great festival in honour of their god, Dagon. The temple was so crowded that three thousand people spilled out onto the roof. There were prayers, songs, dances, poems and plays. Everyone enjoyed themselves immensely. Then people began shouting for Samson to be brought in, so they could mock the former great Israelite chief.

As the huge, blind man was led into the centre of the temple amid jeers, shouts and

133

insults, no one thought anything of the fact that his hair had grown back. And as the crowd booed, hissed and cursed him, no one heard Samson pray, "Oh God, give me back my strength just one last time." Samson stretched out his hands to his right and left and God helped him find the cold marble of the two main pillars of the temple. Then Samson gave a mighty roar. He pushed and heaved and strained. Amid screams and howls of terror, the huge pillars toppled apart and the temple crashed to the ground in ruins.

And so Samson died, taking many thousands of his enemies with him.

Judges chapters 13 to 16

Ruth the Loyal

This is a love story and tells how Ruth found happiness when she married a man called Boaz. He also looked after Ruth's mother-in-law Naomi, who had been left alone when her husband died. Ruth and Boaz are the great-grandparents of David, King of Israel.

Once, there was a terrible famine around Bethlehem. A starving man called Elimelech journeyed with his wife, Naomi, and two sons to live in Moab, where things were better. Then quite suddenly Elimelech died. Naomi and her sons were grief-stricken, but they tried to carry on as Elimelech would have wanted. The boys married, Moabite girls called Ruth and Orpah. But then tragedy struck again – both boys died. Naomi was heartbroken.

"I am going to return home," Naomi told Ruth and Orpah, but Ruth refused to see the old, lonely widow go off on her own. "Where you go, I go," Ruth vowed. "Your people will be my people. Your god, my god."

Naomi smiled gratefully through her tears, and she and Ruth journeyed back to Bethlehem together.

Ruth and Naomi were now very poor. They struggled to make a living. One day, Ruth was in the fields at harvest time, collecting up the leftover corn when she caught the eye of the farm-owner, a man called Boaz. He stopped and asked who she was. Boaz happened to be a cousin of Naomi's and he did what he could to help Ruth. Boaz told her she was welcome in his fields all the time. He told his harvesters to let her drink from their water jars whenever she wanted. He even invited Ruth to join his harvesters for a meal, giving her enough food to take home for supper. Boaz also secretly told his harvesters to leave extra corn behind so Ruth would have more to pick up.

Day after day, Boaz showed Ruth small kindnesses like these, and eventually Naomi dared to send Ruth to ask Boaz formally for his protection.

Boaz was delighted. As was tradition, he went to the city gate and declared in public that he wanted to look after Ruth and Naomi. Boaz and Ruth were married, and Boaz cared for the women all their lives.

So Ruth was rewarded for her loyalty and kindness to Naomi, and Naomi was comforted in her old age. In the fullness of time, God sent Ruth a baby boy, Obed, who brought the two women happiness. They never dreamt that Obed would have a son called Jesse, who would have a son called David, who would one day become the greatest king Israel ever had.

Ruth chapters 1 to 4

Samuel
the Servant

*God was looking for a prophet – someone who would give
His messages to His people on Earth. He looked everywhere
for the right person and finally chose a boy called Samuel to
carry out this important job.*

Samuel was a little boy who lived with
Eli, the high priest at the temple in
Shiloh, where the Ark of the Covenant was
kept. Samuel's mother Hannah had
promised God that her son would serve
Him all his life and learn how to be a priest
one day.

Eli was a good man who looked after
Samuel lovingly. He had two sons of
his own, but they grew up to be
wicked and violent while Samuel
was good and obedient.

One night,
the little boy
was woken
by Eli calling
his name. "Here I am!"
Samuel called, and hurried to see what the
high priest wanted.

"It wasn't me who called you," said Eli,
quite confused. "Go back to bed, son."

But a while later, Samuel was again
woken by Eli calling his name. "Here I am!"
he cried again, and dashed off to find Eli.

"It wasn't me who called you!" Eli reassured Samuel. "Now go back to bed, like a good boy."

But an hour or so later, the voice came again. "Samuel! Samuel!" And Samuel rushed off once more to Eli.

"Samuel," the old high priest said quietly, "I think it must be God who is calling you, and I think you're going to hear Him again. The next time it happens, don't come and find me. Instead call out, 'Speak, Lord, your servant is listening'."

Samuel went back and laid down on his bed in the darkness. And sure enough, the voice came again, "Samuel! Samuel!"

"Speak, Lord, your servant is listening," Samuel replied, just as Eli had told him.

God spoke to Samuel and gave him a difficult message to give the old high priest. A day would come when God was going to punish Israel for its sins and Eli would be punished too, for his sons' wickedness.

In the morning, Samuel was afraid to tell Eli what God had said. When he finally did, the high priest wasn't angry with him. Instead, he hung his head in shame and sadness. "Let God do what He thinks is right," the old man said humbly.

That was the first of many messages that God gave Samuel. For Samuel grew up to be a great prophet who became the ruler of Israel, and was known throughout the land for always speaking the truth.

I Samuel chapters 1 to 3

David and Goliath

When faced with a difficult challenge, David the shepherd boy was strong and fearless. Trusting in God, he stepped up to do battle with the giant Goliath of Gath with just a slingshot and a few stones.

The people of Israel saw that other nations had kings to rule them and demanded that they should have one too. The great prophet Samuel asked God for approval. He was told to choose a man called Saul from the tribe of Benjamin to be the first king of Israel.

King Saul won many victories against
Israel's enemies, but he did not always do as
God wanted. For this reason, God told
Samuel that Saul's sons would never be
king. God ordered that Samuel travel to
Bethlehem and find a shepherd boy called
David, the youngest son of a man called
Jesse. It was David that God wanted to be
the next king. Samuel did so, and gave
David a special blessing, and from then on
God was always with him.

King Saul's army often had to fight the
Philistines because they were constantly
invading Israelite territory. Every Israelite
who could be spared was called to defend
their lands, and three of Jesse's other sons
went to the frontline. One day, Jesse sent

David off with food supplies for them. He reached the camp as a battle was beginning and the armoured soldiers were marching onto the battlefield. Suddenly, they all turned and came running back in fear.

"Whatever is going on?" David called as one terrified soldier ran past.

The man just shouted, "Look!" and pointed behind him.

Striding out in front of the Philistine army was a warrior more enormous than David could have dreamt. He was almost twice as big as everyone else!

"Run away if you like," the giant bellowed.

"There's no need to do battle if you're too cowardly. Just send someone to fight me in single combat. Whoever wins has victory for their side. Now, is any one of you men big enough to take up the challenge?" He smashed his mighty spear against his shield and threw back his head and roared, and the noise crashed around the surrounding hills like thunder.

David was outraged. "How dare he! It's an insult not just to us but to God!" he spat. "Just let me at him! Out in the pastures, I've killed lions and bears when they've attacked my father's flocks and I can do the same to this beast too! God protected me then as He will protect me now."

"Well…" said Saul, casting around for

other volunteers. None were forthcoming.
"Very well, and God be with you." Saul
insisted on dressing David in his own
armour, but it was so big and bulky that he
couldn't move, so David took it off again.
He strode out to meet the giant, Goliath of
Gath, with just his staff, his slingshot and
five smooth stones in his shepherd's pouch.

King Saul and his army watched in
amazement. The giant was roaring with
laughter as a mere child walked towards
him. The young boy was yelling back that
he was going to slay Goliath in the name of
God. The shepherd boy stood firm as the
giant ran towards him with death in his
eyes, brandishing his spear. Then David
raised his slingshot and whirled it around

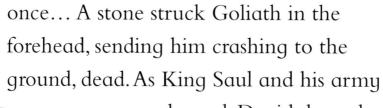

once… A stone struck Goliath in the forehead, sending him crashing to the ground, dead. As King Saul and his army cheered, David drew the giant's sword and cut off Goliath's head with one blow. And the Philistines turned and fled, leaving the Israelites triumphant.

I Samuel chapters 8, 9, 16, 17

Solomon the Magnificent

When David died, his son Solomon became king of Israel. Solomon was famous for his wisdom, wealth and power, and for building a beautiful temple in Jerusalem dedicated to God.

The nation of Israel prospered under King Solomon. He kept peace in his lands and trading routes thrived as merchants could travel in safety. He ruled wisely and well, stunning everyone with his incredible knowledge. Then Solomon began to fulfil his father's dream of building a

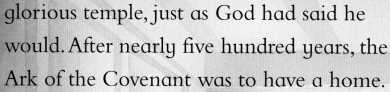

glorious temple, just as God had said he would. After nearly five hundred years, the Ark of the Covenant was to have a home.

Solomon drafted thousands of workers to build the temple. It was made from beautiful cedar wood, which came from the lands of a friend of his, King Hiram of Tyre in Lebanon. Solomon wanted to use only the finest materials and the newest, most exciting techniques, even if it meant going to great lengths and expense to bring materials and craftspeople from abroad. Labourers spent years building massive stone pillars, carving enormous doors and wooden wall panels

with angels and intricate flowers, dying and
weaving beautiful curtains, and lining
whole rooms with gold, which were then
decorated with stunning jewels.

The day finally came when Solomon
ordered the temple to be filled with
treasures and the Ark of the Covenant
brought to its new home. It was done with
such procession and celebrating
that no one had ever seen
anything like it. As the priests
were leaving the temple, the
building was suddenly filled with
a blazing light so bright that
no one could look at it. The
king stood in front of the altar before all of
his people and gave thanks to God, praying

that He would always be with the nation of Israel. Then began a week of feasting.

Solomon didn't stop his building plans at the temple. He erected a magnificent palace and splendid buildings in Jerusalem and Canaan. Rulers from far-off countries travelled to see the marvels for themselves. Even the Queen of Sheba made a journey of fifteen hundred miles through the desert in a camel train laden down with spices, jewels and gold. The queen was amazed – not just by Solomon's incredible buildings but by the wisdom with which he ran the country. "Praise be to your God," she exclaimed, "for He must be hugely pleased with what you have done in His honour."

I Kings chapters 4 to 8, 10

Elijah, Man of God

Elijah was a great prophet who spent his life trying to stop people from worshipping other gods and idols. In a dramatic contest with the prophets of the god Baal, Elijah proved that God was all powerful.

In the days of King Solomon, one way that eastern kings showed their greatness was to have lots of wives. Solomon had one thousand! Most came from abroad, the marriages arranged to seal peace or trade agreements with other rulers. When Solomon married these foreign women, he let them keep the customs of their country, including worshipping strange idols. Many of the wives talked Solomon into worshipping them too. God was so furious at this that He punished Solomon by splitting up the nation of Israel.

When Solomon died, only two of the twelve tribes of Israel asked his son to be their king, and his nation came to be known as Judah. The other ten tribes wanted one of Solomon's advisors to rule them instead – they kept the name of Israel for their nation. Both kings turned out to be bad. They, and many of the kings who came after, forgot to be faithful to God at all. God had to seek out good people to speak for Him, to remind everyone what was right and wrong. The people He chose were called prophets, and one very important one was a man called Elijah.

Elijah lived in Israel when a wicked king called Ahab was on the throne, with his even more wicked queen, Jezebel. They both worshipped the idol Baal and of course the people followed them. God sent Elijah to tell the king how he was going to be punished. "God says there will be no rain or dew in your kingdom for three years," Elijah announced, then he fled from Ahab's fury and hid for the duration of the drought.

God worked miracles to keep Elijah alive as the food ran out and water dried up all over Israel. He even gave Elijah the power to work miracles of his own, such as bringing a dead child back to life.

After three years, God told Elijah to meet King Ahab on the top of Mount Carmel. Elijah told the king to bring the four hundred and fifty prophets of Baal and the four hundred prophets of the false goddess Asherah. "Now let's see who is real and who isn't – Baal and Asherah, or God," Elijah challenged. "Tell your prophets to build an altar and offer a bull as sacrifice to Baal. I'll do the same. Then let us pray for flames to light the sacrificial fire and see who is answered."

And so the king's prophets built an enormous altar and killed a bull. Then they began dancing and singing around it,

calling for Baal to light the fire. All
afternoon they went on, but nothing
happened.

"You might have to sing louder and
dance harder than that," Elijah laughed.
"Perhaps Baal is busy with other things, or
maybe he's gone on a trip, or perhaps he's
asleep?"

Then Elijah got on with
building a little altar to
God for his bull. He
used a bundle
of firewood and
twelve stones
(to represent the tribes of God's Chosen
People). He drenched everything with water
until it was completely soaked and filled the

trench he had dug around it. Then he stood
and said a quiet prayer – a still, lone figure
compared to the hundreds of excited,
chanting prophets of Baal.

Instantly, fire blazed from Heaven and
burned up not just Elijah's bull, but also the
wood, the stones, the earth around about –
everything. Even the trench full of water
hissed and sizzled, and vanished into steam.

The watching crowds fell to the ground
in terror.

Then Elijah told Ahab that all the
prophets of Baal and Asherah should be put
to death, and no one should ever worship
idols again. "By the way," Elijah added
casually, "you should get a move on if you
don't want to get drenched on your way

home." For the skies suddenly darkened with black thunder clouds as God prepared to send Israel rain at last.

God stayed with Elijah for the rest of his life and looked after him. Over the years He spoke many prophecies through him that all came true. God also told Elijah to travel to Syria and find a man called Elisha, whom God wanted as another important prophet. Elijah did so, and Elisha became his constant companion. Elisha was so loyal that he never left his master Elijah's side, even when the time came that the old man knew he was to die.

At that moment, a chariot of fire drawn by blazing horses came thundering towards the two men, forcing them apart. Elijah was

swept up into the chariot and off into the
sky as if by a mighty whirlwind. It circled
higher and higher until it became a tiny
speck and finally disappeared from view.

And so Elijah was gone, leaving behind
only his cloak, lying on the ground.
Elisha picked it up and walked down to
the nearby River Jordan. He lashed
the river with the cloak
and cried out,

"Where is the God of Elijah?" To his astonishment, the waters drew back and parted before him. Then Elisha knew that God was with him as He had been with Elijah, and it was up to him to carry on where Elijah had left off.

I Kings chapters 11, 12, 14 to 19;
II Kings chapter 2

Elisha and the Leper General

*The prophet Elisha carried on with God's work where
Elijah had left off. He was very powerful and could perform
miracles. This story tells how he dealt with a proud general
who suffered from leprosy, and a very greedy servant.*

Elisha the holy man travelled around
Israel, speaking prophecies for God and
working miracles. God gave him so much
power that Elisha even once brought a dead
child back to life, just as his former master,
the prophet Elijah, had done.

News of Elisha's miracles spread far and

wide and all sorts of people, rich and poor, begged him for help. One of them was the commander-in-chief of the Syrian army, General Naaman. He suffered from the terrible skin disease, leprosy. He arrived in his smartest uniform, in a huge convoy of gleaming chariots and bodyguards to see Israel's great miracle worker.

This sort of thing didn't impress Elisha. He didn't even bother to come to the door to see the general. He just sent a servant outside with a message: "Wash in the River Jordan seven times and you will be cured."

Well, General Naaman wasn't used to being treated like that. He huffed about in a terrible temper, shouting things like: "The River Jordan is nothing compared to the

mighty rivers we have back home in Syria!
Why should I wash in a little puddle like
that?" It took all Naaman's men to
calm him down and convince him to
try it.

Six times General Naaman washed
himself in the rushing River Jordan.
When he emerged after the seventh,
his skin was healed.

The overjoyed general hurried back to
Elisha and begged him to accept a fortune
in silver and gold as a thank you. All the
prophet would have was Naaman's
promise to worship God from then on.

However, Elisha's servant Gehazi
was tempted by the sight of the treasure.
When the general set off back to Syria, he

galloped after him and lied
that Elisha had changed his mind
and he would like some money after all.
Naaman delightedly sent Gehazi back with
as much treasure as a couple of his own
servants could carry.

Of course, Elisha mysteriously knew
what Gehazi had done. "You have enough
money now to buy splendid possessions,"
he announced to his servant, "but you
have also bought Naaman's leprosy too."
In horror, Gehazi looked down to see his
hands fester with sores. He stumbled out of
Elisha's house with the skin all over his
body turning white and dead. Gehazi
had been made a leper.

II Kings chapters 4, 5

Jonah and the Whale

God chose Jonah to carry out an important task. But Jonah
tried to run away. He soon found there was no escape and
ended up inside the belly of a huge fish. The fish was so big
that people think it might have been a whale.

One day, God told a man called Jonah,
"Go to Assyria, to the capital city of
Nineveh. Tell the wicked people there about
me and make sure they change their sinful
ways."

Now Jonah didn't care for these people
and wasn't much bothered if they found out

about God or not. He also didn't like the
sound of walking into the capital city of a
powerful, war-like nation and telling the
people what they were doing wrong. So
Jonah got on a boat in the opposite
direction to Nineveh, heading for Spain.

As soon as the ship was on its way, God
sent a mighty storm its way. The sailors on
baord were terrified and began praying to
be saved. Still the rain lashed the boat and
the wind and waves hurled it this way and
that. Then the sailors decided that someone
on board must be cursed. They drew lots
and came up with Jonah's name.
Shamefully, Jonah confessed that he was
disobeying God by being on the boat.
"You'll have to throw me overboard," he

wept, "it's the only way you'll get this storm to stop." The sailors were horrified and did their best to row to shore. But when the storm grew even worse they concluded there was only one thing for it – and dropped Jonah into the water.

The minute they did so, the wind dropped, the rain stopped, the waves died away, and the ship was saved. God saved Jonah too. Instead of letting him sink and drown, He sent a massive fish that swallowed him. For three days Jonah wallowed in the stinky darkness of the fish's belly, praying to God for another chance. Finally, to his relief, the fish spat him out onto a sandy shore.

"Go to Nineveh," God said again, "and give the people my message. If they don't change their behaviour, I will destroy the city after forty days." This time Jonah did what he was told. To his immense surprise the Assyrians listened. The king of Nineveh believed God's threat and ordered his people to mend their ways. Soon, there was a drop in crime. People started being more

polite and kind to each other. They prayed
for forgiveness and fasted, and started
worshipping God. The forty days came and
went and God left the city and its people
untouched.

Jonah stomped off on his own into the
countryside. "I knew this would happen!"
he moaned to God, sitting down in protest.
"I've come all this way – nearly drowned,
been eaten by a fish, then walked for miles
to face crowds of hostile strangers – and all
for nothing. You haven't punished anyone
or destroyed anything at all."

God decided to teach the angry man a
lesson. He made a tree shoot up swiftly
right where Jonah was sitting, so all day he
could rest in its cool shade. However the

next day, God sent insects to eat the tree so it shrivelled and died, leaving Jonah sitting in the blazing sun. God also sent desert wind to roast him. "If only my poor tree hadn't died!" Jonah groaned.

"Well," said God kindly, "if you're upset about a tree – a tree that you neither planted nor looked after – how upset do you think I would have been if the city of Nineveh had been lost? One hundred and twenty thousand people live there, not to mention all the animals."

And Jonah finally understood that God cared for all people, not just the Israelites – and for animals too. After all, hadn't God made them all in the first place?

Jonah

Jeremiah and the End of the Nation

The young prophet Jeremiah knew that the Israelites had displeased God. He showed them what would happen if they didn't mend their ways – like clay in the hands of a potter they could be crushed. But the Israelites would not listen.

Centuries passed and numerous kings came and went on the thrones of Israel and Judah, who had to fight many enemies.

There came a time when the mighty Assyrians rose up against Israel and Judah. The two nations kept the Assyrian empire at bay by paying an enormous amount of treasure each year. However, the emperor eventually sent his armies to attack Israel. God did not stop them because the Israelites had become too sinful to deserve His help. So the Assyrians crushed the ten tribes of God's Chosen People and took them away in their thousands, back to Assyria to be slaves. They filled Israel's capital city of Samaria with captives brought from other lands they had conquered. These settlers became known as Samaritans.

Around one hundred years went by and God chose a young man called Jeremiah to be His prophet in Judah. "You must warn everyone that unless they change their wicked ways, I will send disaster upon them

from the north," God told Jeremiah. God
meant that Judah would be overcome by
another enemy – the Babylonians, who had
become even mightier than the
Assyrians. God sent Jeremiah to
the house of a potter to watch
him shaping clay on his
wheel. "Judah is like clay in
my hands," God explained
to Jeremiah. "If the people do
evil, I will crush them. But if
they do well, I shall mould them
into something good and strong."
Jeremiah told the leaders and people of
Judah many times that it was not too late
for them to mend their ways. However, they
did not listen and God deicided that Judah

would fall. Jeremiah told the people this and he took to wearing a yoke, a harness for an ox, around his neck as a sign to everyone that they would soon be made slaves.

The Judeans hated Jeremiah for his prophecies of destruction, but of course they came true. Nebuchadnezzar, king of Babylon, sent a huge army to attack Judah. The city of Jerusalem was seized and most of the people were taken back to Babylon in chains.

"Do not fear," God told Jeremiah, "when my people in exile repent for their sins, I will bring them out of captivity and restore the kingdom of Israel as a united, great nation once more."

II Kings chapters 17, 18, 25; Jeremiah chapters 1, 18, 24, 27, 31, 39

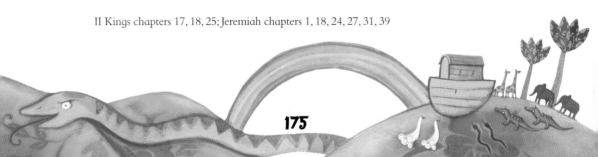

Nebuchadnezzar's Dream

King Nebuchadnezzar was a proud and ruthless man who wanted to rule the world. He was delighted when Daniel was able to tell him the meaning of a strange dream he had about a massive statue of a man.

King Nebuchadnezzar, Emperor of Babylon, was very clever. When he conquered other countries and took their peoples captive, he got his officials to look for those who had special talents so he could put them to good use for himself.

Daniel and his three friends Shadrach,

Meshach and Abednego were among a few young captive Israelite men selected to be trained as advisors to the king. They worked hard and God gave them extra skills as a reward. God made Daniel very good at telling the meaning of dreams and visions.

One morning, the king called an emergency meeting of his advisors. "I have had a worrying dream," Nebuchadnezzar announced, "and I want someone to explain to me what it means."

"Tell us the dream, Your Majesty, and we'll be glad to interpret what it means," replied his advisors, bowing low.

"No," announced Nebuchadnezzar, with a glint in his steely eyes. "You could make up any meaning you like. I want someone

to tell me both the dream and the
meaning. Only then will I be
convinced of the truth."

"And by the way," he added
coldly, "if no one can do it, I'll have
every one of you put to death."

Daniel begged the king for time,
and he, Shadrach, Meshach and
Abednego asked God for help. And so
God sent Daniel a dream, which told
him everything.

"You saw a massive statue," Daniel
told Nebuchadnezzar. "Its head was
gold, its chest and arms silver, its
belly and thighs bronze, its legs
iron and its feet half iron and half clay.
Then an enormous stone bashed against the

statue's feet and the statue toppled and smashed into dust. Then the stone grew into a mountain that covered all the earth.

"This dream means that your empire is like the head of gold, greatest of all. The silver, bronze and iron are three kingdoms that will come after yours, each less powerful than the one before. The last kingdom will be divided into two and will be partly strong and partly weak. But no empire will last until God's kingdom comes and replaces all others forever."

Nebuchadnezzar was astonished and delighted. "Your god must indeed be the god of all gods," he marvelled. He rewarded Daniel and made him chief of his wise men.

Daniel chapters 1, 2

Daniel in the Lions' Den

Daniel loved God and worshipped Him every day, even at a time when it meant breaking the law of the king. When he faced a terrible punishment for his crime, Daniel kept his faith in God – even though he faced death in a den of hungry lions.

When Nebuchadnezzar died, Belshazzar became the new king of Babylon. After him, King Darius of the Medes and Persians seized the throne.

Daniel was such an outstanding advisor that King Darius put him in charge of his empire. The other officials were so jealous that they came up with an idea that would land Daniel in trouble. They suggested to Darius that he should order that no one should pray to anyone but him for thirty days. If anyone disobeyed, they were to be thrown into a pit of lions. The king thought it was a great idea and signed the order.

Now Daniel was a good, holy man. Of course, he continued to pray to God three times a day, as always in front of his window in full view of passers-by.

It wasn't long before his enemies reported him to the king. Darius was devastated, but he could not go back on his word. He ordered for Daniel to be thrown into the den of lions. "May your god save you," the king prayed, and a huge stone was placed over the pit.

Darius spent all night thinking about how he had caused Daniel to be flung to the lions. As soon as dawn came he hurried to the pit and yelled out, "Daniel! Was God with you? Are you still alive?"

To Darius' relief, Daniel answered, "Yes, sire. God sent an angel to guard me and the lions have left me untouched."

The king ordered that Daniel be pulled out of the pit and all the wicked people who had accused him thrown in instead. The lions tore them to bits until nothing but bones were left.

Daniel chapter 6

Queen Esther the Brave

*First, the Babylonians conquered the Israelites, then the
Persians conquered the Babylonians. It was at this time that
the Israelites became known as Jews. Persian King Xerxes
unknowingly chose a Jewish girl, Esther, to be his queen.
She went on to save her people, the Jews, from persecution.*

 King Xerxes was a mighty Persian king
whose empire stretched from India to
Ethiopia. He was once so displeased with
his wife, Vashti, that he announced she was
no longer his queen. He ordered for
beautiful young women to be brought from
all corners of his empire to the palace so he

could choose a new wife.

One of the men who worked in the royal household was an old Jew called Mordecai. He urged his adopted daughter Esther to go to the palace and take part in the beauty competition. Mordecai warned her not to tell anyone she was his daughter or that she was Jewish, for many people hated the captives who had been brought from Israel.

Esther did as she was told and went to the palace. For a year she was pampered with beauty treatments, and had lessons in grooming and how to behave like a queen. When all the candidates were presented to the king, Xerxes chose Esther as his queen. He soon found that she wasn't just a pretty face either. He came to like her very much.

One day, Esther told the king how Mordecai had overheard two servants plotting to kill him, and Xerxes believed Esther at once. He had the two men arrested and hanged, and ordered for the event to be written down in his official Book of Records. Mordecai and Esther had saved his life.

Some time later, King Xerxes made a man called Haman his chief minister and the king commanded his subjects to bow before him. Mordecai always refused. "I bow to none other than God," the old man would insist. This disobedience drove Haman quite mad. He was determined to have revenge. Not just on Mordecai, but on all Jewish people. He told the king that the

Jews were disobedient and nothing but trouble, and that his kingdom would be better off if he had them all put to death. "Whatever you think best," Xerxes told his trusted minister, and gave Haman his royal seal to sign the execution warrant.

When Mordecai found out he was appalled, and begged Esther to ask Xerxes for mercy. She dressed in her finest robes and went unsummoned into the king's presence, an action for which the law said she could have been put to death. Luckily, the king was happy to see her and said she could have whatever she had come for.

"All I would like is for you and Haman to be my guests at dinner tomorrow," Esther said, and the king agreed.

Esther held a wonderful dinner for the men, with delicious food and witty conversation in beautiful surroundings. Having begun to win her husband and his minister over, she invited them to another dinner the following night, when she hoped she could finish the job and ask for forgiveness for the Jews.

Little did she know that later that very evening Haman had ordered that a gallows be built at the palace. They were to hang the man he hated – Mordecai, her father.

At around the same time, Xerxes was
being read aloud to from the Book of
Records. The reader happened to announce
the entry that described how
Mordecai had helped foil the

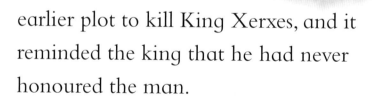

earlier plot to kill King Xerxes, and it
reminded the king that he had never
honoured the man.

Just then, a servant announced that
Haman was asking to see him. He had

come to ask for the king's permission to execute Mordecai.

"Now Haman, tell me what you would do to reward a man you wanted to honour," wondered the king, as his chief minister was ushered in.

Haman tried to hide a smug smirk. He thought that he must be the man the king wanted to honour. "Such a person should be dressed in robes fit for a king and paraded on one of your own horses through the streets as a hero," Haman sighed.

"What a good idea!" Xerxes said, delighted. "Then that's what I want you to do for Mordecai the Jew in the morning."

Haman was outraged, yet he had no choice but to do as the king had

commanded. By the time he arrived at Esther's second supper, Haman's face was as sulky and ugly as Esther's was beautiful.

This time, the queen begged Xerxes for mercy. She confessed that she was a Jew and that orders had been given for all Jewish people to be put to death.

"Who has dared to do such a terrible thing?" boomed the king, outraged.

"The man who is sitting beside you," Esther said quietly. "Haman."

Xerxes was so choked with fury that he couldn't speak and he strode out into the palace gardens.

He returned to find his chief minister at Esther's feet, grabbing at her skirt. Haman was in fact begging for mercy, but it looked as though he was attacking the king's wife. To make matters worse, one of Esther's servants told the king that Haman had built a gallows to kill Mordecai, the very man who had once helped save Xerxes's life.

The king did not delay in having Haman executed on his own gallows. Then he sent letters throughout his empire, ordering that the Jews should be respected, and allowed to defend themselves if necessary.

And that is how the brave, beautiful Esther saved her people, the Israelites.

Esther chapters 1 to 8

People in the Old Testament

Abel Adam and Eve's second son.

Abram (Abraham) A descendant of Noah. God changed his name to Abraham.

Adam The first man on Earth, created by God.

Cain Adam and Eve's first son.

Daniel Among the Israelites taken captive into Babylon. Daniel was thrown to the lions but God saved him from death.

David The youngest son of Jesse, and a shepherd boy. He defeated the giant Goliath of Gath and became the greatest king of Israel.

Esau Isaac and Rebecca's son, and twin brother of Jacob.

Esther An Israelite taken into captivity in Babylon, who became queen to King Xerxes. She saved the Israelites from execution.

Eve The first woman on Earth, created by God.

Jacob The younger of Isaac's and Rebecca's twin boys and brother of Esau.

Jonah An Israelite who was swallowed by a giant fish as a punishment for disobeying God.

Joseph Best-loved son of Jacob. He was sold into slavery by his brothers, but became the King of Egypt's chief minister.

Joshua The leader of the Israelites after Moses, a great commander who conquered most of Canaan – the Promised Land.

Moses An Israelite who grew up as an Egyptian prince. He led the Israelites out of captivity in Egypt.

Nebuchadnezzar The king of the Babylonians.

Noah The man ordered by God to build an ark and load it with creatures and his family when God destroyed the world in a huge flood.

Sarai (Sarah) Abraham's wife. God changed her name to Sarah.

Solomon The son of King David, who became the third king of Israel.